my revision notes

Edexcel GCSE (9–1) History

THE AMERICAN WEST

c.1835–c.1895

Steve May

HODDER EDUCATION
AN HACHETTE UK COMPANY

Dedicated to Chris, Jessica, Hannah, Giacomo, Barry-John, Deia and Vella

The Publishers would like to thank the following for permission to reproduce copyright material.

Photo credit: p15 Granger, NYC/TopFoto.

Every effort has been made to trace all copyright holders, but if any have been inadvertently overlooked, the Publishers will be pleased to make the necessary arrangements at the first opportunity.

Although every effort has been made to ensure that website addresses are correct at time of going to press, Hodder Education cannot be held responsible for the content of any website mentioned in this book. It is sometimes possible to find a relocated web page by typing in the address of the home page for a website in the URL window of your browser.

Hachette UK's policy is to use papers that are natural, renewable and recyclable products and made from wood grown in sustainable forests. The logging and manufacturing processes are expected to conform to the environmental regulations of the country of origin.

Orders: please contact Bookpoint Ltd, 130 Milton Park, Abingdon, Oxon OX14 4SE.
Telephone: +44 (0)1235 827720. Fax: +44 (0)1235 400454. Email education@bookpoint.co.uk
Lines are open from 9 a.m. to 5 p.m., Monday to Saturday, with a 24-hour message answering service.
You can also order through our website: www.hoddereducation.co.uk

ISBN: 978 1 5104 0326 0

© Steve May 2017

First published in 2017 by
Hodder Education,
An Hachette UK Company
Carmelite House
50 Victoria Embankment
London EC4Y 0DZ

www.hoddereducation.co.uk

Impression number   10 9 8 7 6 5 4 3
Year   2021 2020 2019 2018

Cover photo © Eric Isselee/Shutterstock
Illustrations by Gray Publishing
Produced and typeset in Bembo by Gray Publishing, Tunbridge Wells, Kent
Printed in India

A catalogue record for this title is available from the British Library.

How to get the most out of this book

This book will help you to revise for the period study The American West, c.1835–c.1895.

Use the revision planner on pages 2–3 to track your progress, topic by topic. Tick each box when you have:

- revised and understood each topic
- completed the activities
- checked your answers.

The content in the book is organised into a series of double-page spreads which cover the content in the specification. The left-hand page on each spread has the key content for each topic, and the right-hand page has one or two activities to help you with exam skills or to learn the knowledge you need. Answers to these activities can be found at the back of the book on pages 35–38. Quick multiple-choice quizzes to test your knowledge of each topic can be found on the website.

At the end of the book is an exam focus section (pages 29–33) which gives you guidance on how to answer each exam question type.

There are a variety of **activities** for you to complete related to the content on the left-hand page. Some are based on **exam-style questions** which aim to consolidate your revision and practise your exam skills. Others are **revision tasks** to make sure that you have understood every topic and to help you record the key information about each topic.

Tick to track your progress as you revise each element of the key content.

Content for each topic is on the left-hand page.

Shorter **revision tasks** help you to remember key points of content.

Throughout the book there are **exam tips** that remind you of key points that will help you in the exam.

Key terms and **Key individuals** are highlighted in the section colour the first time they appear, with an explanation nearby in the margin. As you work through this book, highlight other key ideas and add your own notes. Make this *your* book.

Contents and revision planner

REVISED

The Great Plains were originally home to the nomadic Plains Indians. Increasing numbers of Americans travelled through and settled on the plains, causing problems and conflicts to develop between the Plains Indians and the settlers.

1 The Plains Indians: their beliefs and way of life

REVISED

1.1 Social and tribal structures

Plains Indians were organised into **bands**, which consisted of between 10 and 50 families, each with its own **tipi**. They travelled, hunted and camped as a band:

- Men were responsible for hunting, tending the horses and protecting the band. Women were responsible for cooking, looking after the tipi and making clothes.
- Women also had a key responsibility to raise children.
- Old people were valued for their wisdom and experience.

The bands met at least once a year as a Nation. Important decisions were made at this council meeting.

1.2 Ways of life and means of survival

The horse was essential to the way of life and survival of the Plains Indians:

- It allowed them to be **nomadic**; it was used for transport and warfare.
- The horse also signified status as horsemanship was a measure of bravery, and the number of horses owned was a measure of wealth.

The buffalo was also essential to Plains Indians' survival:

- The Plains Indians conducted a buffalo dance to call the spirits to help them hunt buffalo.
- The hunt was carefully organised by warrior societies, and the stampede and eventual kill were also carefully managed.
- Once dead, the buffalo was butchered, with some parts eaten raw and others boiled, roasted, or smoked and preserved.
- The buffalo hide was used for clothing and tipi covers.

1.3 Beliefs about land

The Plains Indians believed that spirits had created the world and all life. The **Sioux** people believed that they came from the land, and when they died they should be returned to the land. Some land was sacred, especially high land as it was closer to the spirits. The land was not owned by anyone.

1.4 Attitudes to war and property

To the Plains Indian, war was not about a long-fought campaign resulting in a victor and a peace treaty. It was a series of raids by small groups with a purpose, for example stealing horses, seeking revenge or securing hunting grounds. War did not happen in the cold winter months; it was a summer activity after food supplies had been built up by hunting.

Plains Indians took scalps as evidence of their success in war. Scalps were dried and hung outside tipis as trophies. If a warrior lost his scalp he could not go to the afterlife (the place Indians went to after their death). Even after guns became part of warfare, it was more important to the Plains Indian to get so close to the enemy that you could touch him; this became known as '**counting coup**'.

> **Key terms**
>
> **Band** A small group of Plains Indians made up of several families
>
> **Counting coup** The winning of prestige against an enemy through acts of bravery
>
> **Nomadic** Living the life of a nomad, with no fixed home; wandering
>
> **Sioux** One of the Indian Nations that were Plains Indians
>
> **Tipi** A tent made from buffalo skins and wooden poles

> **Exam tip**
>
> You will need to know that the main beliefs of the Plains Indians were very different from those of the new American settlers.

Organising knowledge

Use the information on page 4 to complete the table below to summarise the key factors in Plains Indians' beliefs and way of life.

Key factor	Impact on Plains Indians' beliefs and way of life
The role of men, women and old people	
The horse	
The buffalo	
The land	
War	

Adding a third factor

To answer the narrative question (see page 31), you need to explain three developments. It is sensible to make use of the two given points. However, you will need to explain a third development. Look at the exam-style question below and write down your choice for a third development. Give reasons why you have chosen it.

Write a narrative account of the beliefs and way of life of the Plains Indians at the time of the early settlement of the West, c.1835–c.1862.

You may use the following in your answer:
- Social and tribal organisation
- The importance of animals in daily life and for survival

You **must** also use information of your own.

Third development: _____

_____

Why I have chosen this: _____

_____

_____

Details to support this point: _____

_____

_____

_____

1 The Plains Indians: their beliefs and way of life (cont.) REVISED

1.5 US government policy

The early history of the relationship between the Plains Indians and the people from the founding colonies of the USA ranged from friendship and cooperation to open hostility and war. The Indian Nations were destroyed as settlers moved across the Great Plains.

Reservations

- At the beginning, the settlers negotiated with the Indian Nations. The Native Americans surrendered some of their lands to the USA and were given other lands called **reservations**.

- Over time, the term reservation was used to describe any area of land on which the Plains Indians were confined, whether they had originally lived there or not.

- In 1824, the Bureau of Indian Affairs was set up, within the US War Department, to manage the relationship with the Plains Indians.

The Indian Removal Act 1830

- In 1830, the Indian Removal Act established a Permanent Indian Frontier.

- This was a boundary between the USA and Indian Territory, and removed many Indian Nations from the south-west to the Indian Territory, which now shrank in size until it was what later became the state of Oklahoma.

- These actions were taken supposedly for the protection of the Plains Indians, but in effect, it forced the removal of thousands of Plains Indians.

- The removal became known as 'The Trail of Tears'; it was completed by 1838.

- Plains Indians were marched more than 1500 km, with many dying of starvation, whooping cough, typhus, dysentery and cholera.

The Indian Appropriations Act 1851

- By the early 1850s, settlers were moving beyond the Permanent Indian Frontier to the eastern edges of the Great Plains.

- The US government encouraged this westwards movement but also realised that the Plains Indians needed protection.

- The Bureau of Indian Affairs had now been moved from the War Department to the Department of the Interior, as US government policy focused on trying to 'civilise' the Plains Indians by confining them to reservations and setting up schools.

- The outcome of this was the Indian Appropriations Act 1851, which set up legally recognised Indian reservations, as a way of protecting the Plains Indians.

Key term

Reservation Land set aside for Plains Indians to live on

Revision task

What part was played by the following policies in worsening relations between Plains Indians and the US colonists?

- the creation of reservations
- the Indian Removal Act 1830
- the Indian Appropriations Act 1851.

Exam tip

Make sure that you know in what ways the government supported westward expansion while at the same time diminishing both the territory and the independence of the Plains Indians.

✎ How important

Complete the table below.

- Briefly summarise why each factor was important to the Plains Indians' way of life.
- Make a decision about the importance of each factor in determining how Plains Indians lived. Give a brief explanation for each choice.

Factor	Key features	Decisive	Important	Quite important
Living as a band				
The horse				
The buffalo				
Belief in spirits				
Attitude to war				
The role of the US government				

✎ Improving your answer

Plan an answer to the question below. Compare your plan with that of another student and suggest three ways in which the plan could be improved.

Write a narrative account analysing US government policy towards Plains Indians.

> You may use the following in your answer:
> - Indian Removal Act 1830
> - Indian Appropriations Act 1851
>
> You **must** also use information of your own.

My plan

2 Migration and early settlement

2.1 The factors encouraging migration

Manifest Destiny

Many Americans believed that their country should occupy the entire continent, from the east coast on the Atlantic to the west coast on the Pacific. This view, which became known as **Manifest Destiny**, encouraged the belief that it was the 'God-given duty' of Americans to spread 'civilisation' and 'democracy'. The phrase was first employed by John L. O'Sullivan in an article on the annexation of Texas.

Manifest Destiny expressed the belief that it was Anglo-Saxon Americans' mission to expand their civilisation and institutions across the breadth of North America. Many people saw in this belief a strong racial element which suggested that America was the land of white people, and it was they who should govern it and populate it.

Economic depression

In 1837, the USA was hit by an **economic depression**:

- In the East, banks collapsed and savings were lost; wages were cut and jobs lost.
- High unemployment drove people in the East to look to move westwards in the hope of finding a better life.

News of unsettled fertile land in Oregon and California reached the East. Farmers in the Mississippi valley struggled as the economic depression drove down prices for wheat and corn. The chance of farming in Oregon and California seemed very attractive:

- The challenge of 'life on the frontier' of American expansion attracted many who had a sense of daring and adventure.
- In 1842, the US government encouraged settlers to stake a claim for the ownership of land by introducing the Pre-emption Act, which allowed them to buy 160 acres of land for $1.25 an acre.
- With victory over Mexico in 1848, California became part of the USA, and this encouraged settlers to move there.
- In 1846, the Oregon Treaty with Britain saw Oregon become part of the USA, and this was now accessible and attractive to settlers.
- The discovery of the South Pass through the Rockies, by 'mountain men', enabled settlers to reach areas like Oregon and California.

The Gold Rush of 1849

- Miners who moved west went in search of gold, and became known as the 'forty-niners'.
- They were not seeking the solitary life of the 'mountain men', or the fertile farmland of the settlers, or freedom from persecution. They wanted wealth.
- In 1848, news of the discovery of gold in the foothills of California's Sierra Nevada mountains spread like wildfire, and by 1849, miners were arriving not only from across America, but also from around the world, including China.

> **Key terms**
>
> **Economic depression**
> An economic decline leading to a fall in living standards
>
> **Manifest Destiny**
> The belief of the non-native American people that it was their God-given duty to settle across the whole of North America

> **Exam tip**
>
> Ensure that you understand the factors encouraging migration to the West as well as those factors pushing people from the East.

Memory map

Create a memory map to show how the different factors considered on page 8 encouraged migration west. Add some key words from the information on page 8 and your own knowledge to the diagram opposite. Use three different colours to show which factors are political, economic or person challenges. To help you remember the information you could add small drawings.

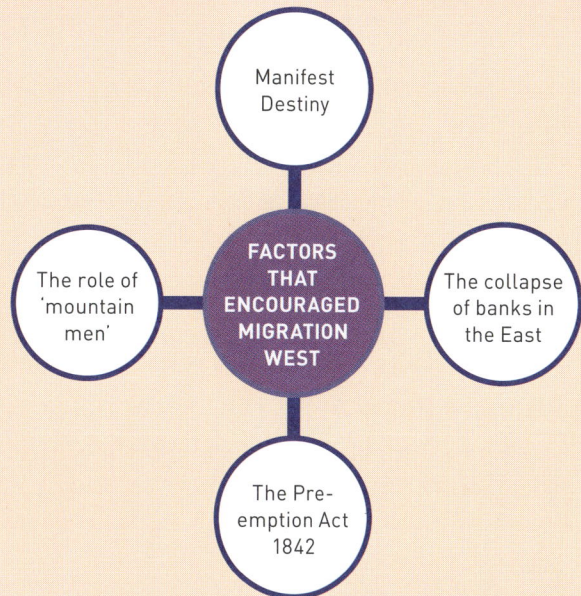

Manifest Destiny

FACTORS THAT ENCOURAGED MIGRATION WEST

The role of 'mountain men'

The collapse of banks in the East

The Pre-emption Act 1842

Concentric circles

In the concentric circles, rank order the following reasons that encouraged migration west, from the most important in the middle to the least important on the outside. Explain your decisions. Are there any links between the reasons? If so, indicate these on the circles with arrows and explain the links.

- searching for space
- economic depression
- government encouragement
- political ideas.

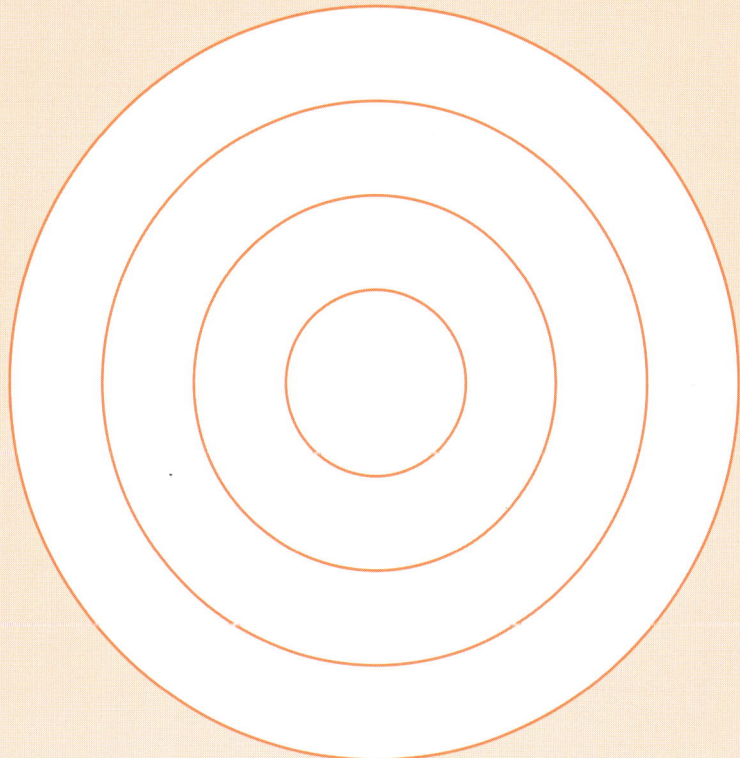

2 Migration and early settlement (cont.)

2.2 The process and problems of migration

The four-month journey from the East to Oregon or California was long and hazardous:

- Many migrating families faced a series of hazards in an attempt to get to their destination more quickly. For example, the Hastings Cutoff was an untested route through the Wasatch Mountains and the Great Salt Desert that led to the Sierra Nevada.
- Food supplies ran low as journeys took longer than expected, despite the use of supposed short cuts. Some settlers resorted to cannibalism in order to survive.

The Donner Party

- The Donner Party (led by the Donner brothers, Jacob and George) set off from Independence, Missouri, in May 1846, heading for California. By June they had reached Little Sandy River.
- The Donners, and others, then decided to head for Fort Bridger and take the Hastings Cutoff, rather than follow a more established route.
- The Donner Party lost four wagons, many oxen and cattle and, more importantly, a whole month's time.
- As they crossed the Sierra Nevada mountain range, the snow came and the Donner Party became stranded.
- By mid-December their food supplies were running low and people began to die.
- A small group of seventeen men, women and children had left on foot, with seven of them eventually making it to California.
- Of the 87 original members of the Donner Party, 46 survived to eventually reach California, many of them having eaten the dead to survive.

The Mormon migration, 1846–47

The main motive for the **Mormon** migrants was neither the acquisition of land nor gold, but to escape from persecution due to their religious beliefs and their acceptance of **polygamy**. More than 16,000 Mormons crossed the Great Plains and many settled in an area that became known as Salt Lake City.

The Gold Rush

The discovery of gold in California in 1848 attracted the migration of many who were unprepared for the journey but greedy for the promise of wealth. This created the **Gold Rush**. The Gold Rush led to the population of California increasing from 15,000 to 250,000 by 1852. This brought problems like violence and lawlessness.

2.3 White settlement farming

White settlers faced many problems such as water shortages, extremes of weather, lack of fuel, a shortage of building materials, and dirt and disease. These problems affected their livelihood, which was farming:

- Crops failed because of a shortage of water, extreme heat in the summer led to drought, and extreme cold in the winter damaged or destroyed crops.
- The grasslands of the plains proved difficult to plough, and with little wood there was no way of protecting growing crops from straying animals and buffalo.
- The **prairie** lands of the plains were also susceptible to wildfire which would destroy crops, and were also plagued by grasshoppers which would eat crops.

Key terms

Gold Rush A rapid movement of people to a newly discovered goldfield

Mormon A member of the Church of Jesus Christ of Latter-day Saints, founded in 1830 by Joseph Smith

Polygamy Having more than one wife at the same time

Prairie A large area of open grassland

Quick quizzes at **www.hoddereducation.co.uk/myrevisionnotes**

Organising knowledge

Use the information on page 10 to complete the table below to summarise the problems encountered when migrating.

Factors	Major problem	Minor problem
The time migration took		
Encountering hazards		
Food supplies		
Being unprepared		
Increasing the population of an area		

In the balance

Using the information on page 10, complete both sides of the scales to show whether migration was worth the journey.

Do you think that migration was worth the journey? Give reasons for your answer.

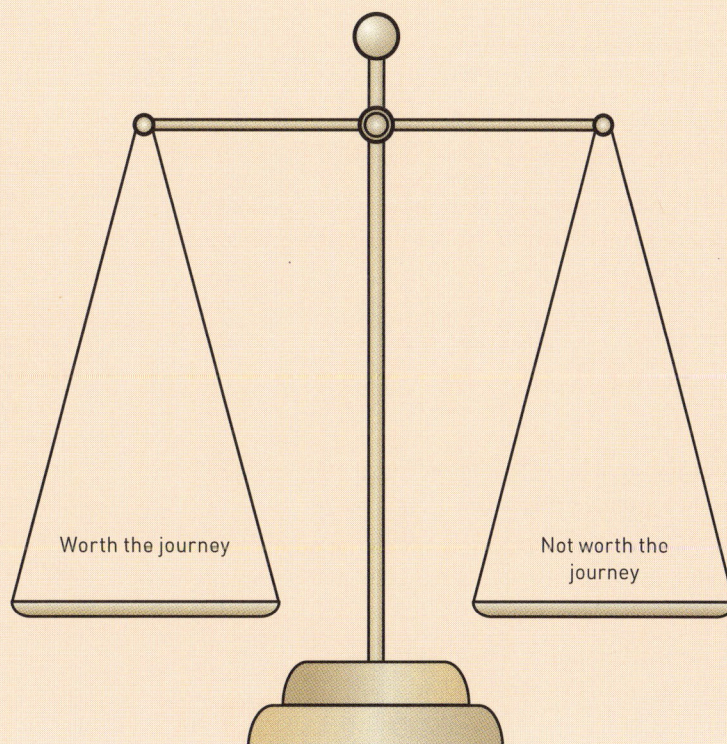

Worth the journey

Not worth the journey

3 Conflict and tension

3.1 Tension between settlers and Plains Indians

As the settlers crossed the Great Plains they affected the lives of the Plains Indians. The settlers made use of already scarce water supplies and frightened away the animals that the Plains Indians hunted. The settlers also brought with them an epidemic of **smallpox** which spread across the Plains during 1837–39.

3.2 The Fort Laramie Treaty 1851

In an attempt to stop conflict and tension between the settlers and the Plains Indians from escalating, the US government created the Fort Laramie Treaty. The treaty was agreed between the government and representatives of the Plains Indian Nations (Arapaho, Cheyenne, Crow and Sioux):

- The treaty separated the two sides through the creation of reservations and hunting areas.
- The Plains Indians promised not to attack travelling settlers and to allow the building of roads and forts, in return for an annual subsidy.
- The treaty did not please everybody. Some of the Indian Nations did not feel bound by it, and a group of Americans called the 'exterminators', who saw the Native Americans as savages, wanted a military solution which would wipe out the Plains Indians.

3.3 The problems of lawlessness

The new settler towns (many of them based on gold and silver mining) that sprang up as a consequence of migration saw significant lawlessness. Key reasons for this lawlessness are:

- the absence of family life
- the easy and uncontrolled availability of alcohol
- the practice of carrying weapons
- the frontier code which asserted that a man had the right to stand his ground and defend what he had with the use of weapons if necessary.

Lawlessness showed itself in highway robbery, rowdy and drunken behaviour, conflict between groups of settlers and Plains Indians, killings based on an argument or disagreement and **vigilante** action.

3.4 Attempts to tackle lawlessness

Towns attempted to manage this lawlessness in a variety of ways and with varying success:

- The **county sheriff** was responsible for law enforcement and tax collection. He ran the county jail and appointed **deputies**.
- The **township constable** or **city marshal** was an elected official responsible for law enforcement within town or city boundaries. He ran the town or city jail.
- Some towns had their own **militia** units. These were local men, who were armed, and they managed law enforcement.
- There were courts that investigated crime and death, and there was a **Grand Jury** whose role was to investigate public offences and hand down **indictments**.

Key terms

City marshal The elected chief law enforcement officer of a city or town

County sheriff An elected official who is in charge of enforcing the law in a US county

Deputy A person who is appointed to undertake the duties of a superior in the superior's absence

Grand Jury A jury, normally of 23 jurors, selected to examine the validity of an accusation prior to trial

Indictment A formal charge or accusation of a serious crime

Militia A military force that is raised from the civil population to supplement a regular army in an emergency

Smallpox A contagious viral disease, with fever and pustules that usually leave scars

Township constable A public officer, usually of a town, responsible for keeping the peace

Vigilante Member of a self-appointed group of citizens who undertake law enforcement in their community without legal authority, typically because the legal agencies are thought to be inadequate

Exam tip

Ensure that you understand the conflict between settlers and Plains Indians and the promises made on both sides. You will need to know the significance of the Fort Laramie Treaty.

In the balance

Using the information on page 12, copy and complete both sides of the scales to show whether Plains Indians were better or worse off.

Do you think Plains Indians were better or worse off overall? Give reasons for your answer.

Better off   Worse off

Develop the detail

Below are an exam-style question and a paragraph which is part of the answer to the question. The paragraph states the importance of the Fort Laramie Treaty of 1851 but this is not supported with sufficient evidence. Complete the paragraph by adding more detail about the importance of the Fort Laramie Treaty of 1851.

Explain **two** of the following:

- The importance of the Fort Laramie Treaty 1851.

- The importance of lawlessness in the development of settler towns.

- The importance of attempts to tackle lawlessness.

The Fort Laramie Treaty was an attempt to stop conflict and tension between the settlers and the Plains Indians from escalating. The treaty was agreed between the US government and representatives of the Plains Indian Nations (Arapaho, Cheyenne, Crow and Sioux).

_____

_____

_____

_____

Now complete answers to the other two bullet points.

Key topic 2 Development of the plains, c.1862–c.1876

The process of settlement of the plains accelerated and this was aided by the building of railroads. Conflict and tension continued and lawlessness spread. The consequences of the American Civil War also played their part in plains development.

1 The development of settlement in the West

REVISED

1.1 The significance of the Civil War

As the **American Civil War** was being fought (1861–65), it created problems for the development of the West:

- During the war, regular troops were withdrawn from service in the West and replaced with volunteer militia. This had a disastrous impact on settler relations with the Plains Indians.

- The war also slowed down the rate at which settlers were moving west, as the war caused disruption, destruction and damage to railroad tracks.

- When the war ended in 1865, more money became available through 'reconstruction' to help develop the West further.

Building of the **Central Pacific Railroad** started in 1865, opening up further opportunities for settlers to move west. To maximise its income, the railroad company encouraged settlers (homesteaders) to settle along the line.

In May 1869, the transcontinental railroad, connecting the rail lines of the Central Pacific and the Union Pacific was completed. The workforce needed feeding, and the buffalo was a good source of fresh meat. William Cody, who later became better known as 'Buffalo Bill', reportedly killed 4280 buffalo. The impact on the Plains Indians was significant.

The **Southern Homestead Act 1866**, the **Timber Culture Act 1873** and the **Desert Land Act 1877** all gave settlers right to acquire land cheaply and further encouraged settlement in the West.

Revision task

Make a list of the government incentives which encouraged settlers to move west. Now annotate the list with details about how each action or policy was effective in enabling settlers to benefit from moving west.

Exam tip

You will already know that the ending of the Civil War brought new settlers to the plains but you should also know about the government incentives which encouraged settlers to move west.

Key terms

American Civil War The war between the northern US states (usually known as the Union) and the Confederate States of America, 1861–65

Central Pacific Railroad The former name of the railroad network built between California and Utah, USA that formed part of the 'First Transcontinental Railroad' in North America

Desert Land Act 1877 To encourage and promote the economic development of the arid and semiarid public lands of the Western states

Southern Homestead Act 1866 A US federal law enacted to break a cycle of debt during the Reconstruction following the American Civil War

Timber Culture Act 1873 Allowed homesteaders to get another 160 acres (0.65 km²) of land if they planted trees on one-fourth of the land, because the land was 'almost one entire plain of grass, which is and ever must be useless to cultivating man'

Contemporary cartoon commemorating the 1869 joining of the Central Pacific and Union Pacific Railroads.

✏ Adding a third factor

To answer the narrative question (see page 31), you need to explain three developments. It is sensible to make use of the two given points. However, you will need to explain a third development. Look at the exam-style question below and write down your choice for a third development. Give reasons why you have chosen it.

Write a narrative account analysing the significance of the American Civil War on the development of the Great Plains in the years c.1862–c.1876.

> You may use the following in your answer:
> - The destruction to railroad tracks caused by the war
> - The money available at the end of the war for 'reconstruction'
>
> You **must** also use information of your own.

Third development: _____

_____

Why I have chosen this: _____

_____

Details to support this point: _____

_____

_____

_____

✏ Understanding the chronology

Place the events between 1861 and 1876 listed below in the correct chronological sequence in the timeline.

Date	Event
1861–65	
1865	
1866	
1869	
1873	
1877	

A Completion of the transcontinental railroad
B Southern Homestead Act
C Desert Land Act
D Timber Culture Act
E The American Civil War
F Building of the Central Pacific Railroad started

1 The development of settlement in the West (cont.)

1.2 Problems faced by homesteaders

The homesteaders who had managed to stay long enough gradually began to deal with some of the problems that made life in the West so difficult. However, they still faced a number of natural hazards.

Some areas of land in the Great Plains were simply less fertile than other areas and had the additional problems of high winds, low rainfall, harsh winters, and grasshopper and locust swarms.

Overcoming the problems

Nevertheless, some homesteaders became prosperous and moved beyond a subsistence existence:

- They built windmills, which gave them power to pump water and irrigate land.
- They developed a method called 'dry farming' that trapped moisture in the soil. They developed new crops, for example hard winter wheat, that could survive and grow in the Great Plains.
- John Deere invented a strong steel plough which could cut through the prairie grass.
- Railways brought building materials, particularly wood.
- Barbed wire was invented in 1874, providing a cheap and effective way to fence in, and protect, cattle and other livestock.

1.3 Continued problems of law and order

Lawlessness continued to be a problem because its root causes had not been sufficiently dealt with:

- Weapons continued to be owned without licence, conflict between groups and the Plains Indians remained, and the West was too big a geographical area to police and enforce laws.
- The movement of people west by stagecoach encouraged the continued activity of highway and stagecoach robberies.
- Some **ex-Confederate soldiers** turned to bank robbery. The **James–Younger gang** became the most famous and notorious bank and stagecoach robbers.
- Train robbery became more prevalent with the growth of the railways, forcing rail companies to take countermeasures.

Key terms

Ex-Confederate soldier
A supporter of, and fighter for, the Confederate States of America during the Civil War

James–Younger gang
A notable nineteenth-century gang of American outlaws that included Jesse James

Revision task

Make a list of the problems faced by homesteaders who settled in the West. For each problem note down at least one way in which homesteaders attempted to combat these difficulties.

Exam tip

Ensure that you understand the problems with law and order, as well as the range of difficulties faced by homesteaders in living and farming the land.

Consequences and importance

Make a copy of the following table and explain the consequences and importance of each problem faced by homesteaders.

Problem	Consequences	Importance
Location of their land		
High winds		
Low rainfall		
Natural hazards		
Cold winters		
Ownership of weapons		

Organising knowledge

Use the information on pages 14 and 16 to complete the table below to summarise the key changes in the settlement of the West between 1862 and 1877.

Factor	1862	1877
Railroad transportation		
Farming		
Law and order		
Land acquisition rights		

2 Ranching and the cattle industry

2.1 The growth of the cattle industry

The American Civil War played a part in the development of the cattle industry. Texan cattle ranchers, who had fought for the South, returned to find their cattle herds had grown dramatically. Therefore, cattle were not worth much unless they were sold, and to do this they had to be 'driven' to markets in the eastern states. The railroads provided a means of transporting cattle east, so cattle were driven to towns on the railway routes. Abilene became a key cattle or 'cow' town, and towns like it prospered.

Abilene

From 1868, the cattle drives brought prosperity to Abilene and its citizens. With prosperity also came problems of law and order. After months of driving cattle, **cowboys** had money in their pockets and wanted to celebrate once they hit town. They spent their money in Abilene's saloons, at gambling tables and at brothels. Abilene's prosperity started to wane when local resistance to the cattle drives pushed them further west along new trails.

2.2 Changes in the work of the cowboy

- The original cowboys were the Spanish *vaqueros* in Texas. Cowboys were men who worked with cattle on the cattle drives and in the ranches. They were skilled in horsemanship.
- Their job entailed line riding, which meant patrolling the boundaries of the ranch for strays and **branding** cattle. It was a lonely job and not well paid.
- As more and more cattle were driven to markets in the East, the cowboy's role was focused on managing the herd on its journey to a cow town for transportation.

Iliff, Goodnight and McCoy

- John Iliff was one of the earliest cattle ranchers, having failed to strike it rich as a gold miner. He realised that cattle could survive the winter on the plains. He eventually had a herd of over 35,000 beef cattle, selling meat to the railroad builders.
- Charles Goodnight discovered that Texan longhorn cattle could survive the winter on the plains and that the cold weather killed disease-carrying ticks that lived off the cattle. He experimented further with cattle breeding and produced better quality meat.
- Joseph McCoy was also a cattle rancher who bought land, built stock pens and advertised Abilene as a cattle shipping point.

2.3 Rivalry between ranchers and homesteaders

This movement of cattle annoyed homesteaders, who resisted, and quite often forced cattle drives along new trails away from their land. From 1865 onwards, wealthy and powerful ranchers used force to move settlers off their land or charge them high rents. If necessary, they used cowboys and guns.

> **Key terms**
>
> **Branding** Marking cattle with a red-hot iron to indicate ownership
>
> **Cowboy** A man who herds and tends cattle, performing much of his work on horseback

> **Exam tip**
>
> Remember you will need to give examples from the range of factors and the achievements of individuals which affected the cattle industry, ranching and the work of cowboys.

✏ Identifying consequences

Below is an exam-style question.

Explain two consequences of the growth in the cattle industry.

In answering this question, it is important that you focus on consequence. In the table below are statements about the cattle industry. Identify (with a tick in the appropriate column) whether they are causes, events or consequences of the growth in the cattle industry.

Statement	Cause	Event	Consequence
The Civil War played a part in the growth of the cattle industry			
Cattle ranchers who had fought in the war returned to find that their herds had grown significantly in size			
Cattle were worth less after the war and had to be sold			
Cow towns emerged and became prosperous			
The work of the cowboys changed as they now drove cattle to a town for transportation			

✏ In the balance

Using the information on page 18, copy and complete both sides of the scales to show whether cowboys were better or worse off because of the growth in the cattle industry.

Do you think cowboys were better or worse off overall than before the growth of the cattle industry? Give reasons for your answer.

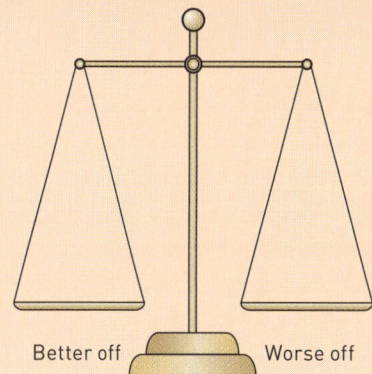

Better off   Worse off

3 Changes in the way of life of the Plains Indians

3.1 Railroads, the cattle industry and gold prospecting

- The advance of the railroads across the Great Plains disrupted the hunting grounds of the Plains Indians and significantly threatened their way of life.
- Buffalo provided a much-needed source of meat for railroad builders. Also, hunting buffalo became a 'white man's sport', and special trains were run for buffalo shoots.
- The leather industry benefited as the railroads transported hides back to the East.
- The development of cattle ranching meant that land where the buffalo had once roamed and grazed was now fenced off, decreasing buffalo numbers.
- The effects of gold **prospecting** varied. In California, the Native American population was wiped out; in other areas prospecting led to increased tension and conflict.

3.2 US government policy

- In 1862, when gold prospectors left the **Oregon Trail** and crossed Sioux lands, breaking the existing Peace Treaty (see page 12), the US government took no action.
- In 1867, to try to end the fighting because of the **Sand Creek Massacre** of 1864, the US government set up a peace commission. The Arapaho and Cheyenne were presented with a choice: move to a reservation or be seen as hostile.
- In 1868, the US government agreed to the second Fort Laramie Treaty, creating the **Great Sioux Reservation**, and rerouting the trails to gold-mining territories.
- In 1869, President **Ulysses Grant** recognised that the wars of **extermination** had been unacceptable and advanced a peace policy. Reservations would have government funding for education, and the army was to defend the reservations rather than simply let them be attacked.
- In 1871, the Indian Appropriations Act ended the treatment of Native Americans as separate nations, and they were now treated as individuals or as wards of the state.

3.3 Conflict with the Plains Indians

Little Crow's War, 1861–62

The Santee Sioux Reservation was not suitable for farming, and Native Americans were forced to live on **credit**. Violence erupted and settlers were killed. The army moved in and the Santee Sioux surrendered.

The Cheyenne Wars, 1864–67

These were sparked by the discovery of gold in Colorado. The area of Pikes Peak was a Native American hunting ground, but mining settlements allowed settlers to move across the land. There were outbreaks of fighting and the army moved in. A peace commission was set up in 1867 to try to end the fighting. The Arapaho and Cheyenne were presented with a choice: move to a reservation or been seen as hostile. The chiefs signed the Treaty of Medicine Lodge, agreeing to move to a reservation.

> **Key terms**
>
> **Credit** An amount of money extended to a borrower, so the borrower pays nothing immediately
>
> **Extermination** Killing of a whole group of people
>
> **Great Sioux Reservation** The original area of land encompassing what is today South Dakota and Nebraska
>
> **Oregon Trail** The route over which settlers travelled to Oregon. It passed through what is now Missouri, Kansas, Nebraska, Wyoming and Idaho
>
> **Prospecting** Searching for sites where gold could be found
>
> **Sand Creek Massacre** In 1864, 1000 militia men from the Colorado Volunteers attacked a Cheyenne village, despite a white flag and a US flag being flown by the Cheyenne chief

> **Key individual**
>
> **Ulysses Grant** Eighteenth US president. As commanding general, Grant worked closely with President Abraham Lincoln to lead the Union Army to victory over the Confederacy in the American Civil War

Red Cloud's War, 1866–68

The discovery of gold in Sioux lands led to miners and settlers crossing Sioux hunting grounds. The Sioux attacked travellers but were not strong enough to attack forts. The Sioux lost heavily in the fights but, at times, so did the US Army. The US government realised that it could not defeat the Sioux without sending in greater numbers of soldiers and so the 1868 Fort Laramie Treaty was signed. In this treaty, the US government recognised the Black Hills as part of the Great Sioux Reservation, set aside for exclusive use by the Sioux people.

Consequences and importance

Make a copy of the following table and explain the consequences and importance of each factor in changing the life of the Plains Indians. You may want to look at page 20 for more information.

Factor	Consequences	Importance
The advance of the railroad		
Cattle ranches		
Gold prospecting		
Indian Appropriations Act 1871		
The Cheyenne Wars 1864–67		

Adding a third factor

To answer the narrative question (see page 31), you need to explain three developments. It is sensible to make use of the two given points. However, you will need to explain a third development. Look at the exam-style question below and write down your choice for a third development. Give reasons why you have chosen it.

Write a narrative account analysing US government policy towards the Plains Indians in the years 1862–76.

You may use the following information in your answer:
- The Fort Laramie Treaty 1868
- The 'Peace Policy' of President Ulysses Grant

You **must** also use information of your own.

Third development: _____

Why I have chosen this: _____

Details to support this point: _____

Key topic 3 Conflicts and conquest, c.1876–c.1895

During this period, people struggled to thrive, to survive and to preserve their way of life. There was tension and conflict between competing economic groups, between the forces of law and order, and between the US government and the Plains Indians.

1 Changes in farming, the cattle industry and settlement REVISED ☐

1.1 Changes in farming

- The expansion of the railroads brought about significant improvements in farming.
- Homesteaders were able to buy a wide range of farming machinery, for example binders, reapers and threshers, at cheaper prices, and they could buy spares.
- **James Oliver** improved steel ploughs, enabling farmers to cultivate more land.
- Increased crop yields led to more money, which then led to further investment in better technology.
- However, homesteaders could not control the weather, and severe droughts in the 1870s and 1880s led to bankruptcies.
- Nevertheless, by the 1890s, the Great Plains had become more fertile and many homesteaders prospered.

> **Key individual**
>
> **James Oliver** An inventor and industrialist who improved the sod-buster plough, invented by John Deere, which enabled farmers to bring more land under cultivation

1.2 Changes in the cattle industry

Cattle ranching had developed because the railways allowed cattle to be transported to markets in the East. However, shipping live cattle further afield was inefficient as much of the animal was inedible. The development of refrigerated railcars solved the problem. Meat could now be transported over greater distances:

- More and more cattle were demanded and this put pressure both on their price and on the stock of grass that was available for them to graze.
- The winter of 1886–87 was so cold that thousands of cattle died. The 'open range' had had its best days and the boom was over. It was replaced by smaller ranches, and cowboys' lives were never the same again.

1.3 Continued growth of settlement

The Exoduster movement

In the 1870s, black Americans, many of whom had been freed from slavery at the end of the Civil War, looked to escape poverty, racism, intimidation and attacks by the Ku Klux Klan. They became known as the Exodusters, and looked to settle in Kansas.

The Oklahoma Land Rush, 1893

The first Oklahoma Land Rush came in 1889 when the federal government opened up for settlement 2 million acres of land in Oklahoma. It had been part of the Indian Territory, and contained some of most fertile land in the West. The second land rush that followed in 1893 was the largest America had ever seen. People were carried there by all kinds of transportation, racing to claim an estimated 100,000 plots of land, previously known as the Cherokee Strip.

Many would be disappointed, as there were only 42,000 plots of land available. Also, many of the plots had already been claimed by 'Sooners', who had sneaked into the land claim area before the race began. Once the rush was over, the land was transformed for the better by the settlers.

Quick quizzes at **www.hoddereducation.co.uk/myrevisionnotes**

Concentric circles

In the concentric circles opposite, rank order the following reasons why farming changed in the years c.1876–c.1895, from the most important in the middle to the least important on the outside. Explain your decisions.

- expansion of the railroads
- improved farming equipment
- farming machinery was cheaper
- the Great Plains had become more fertile.

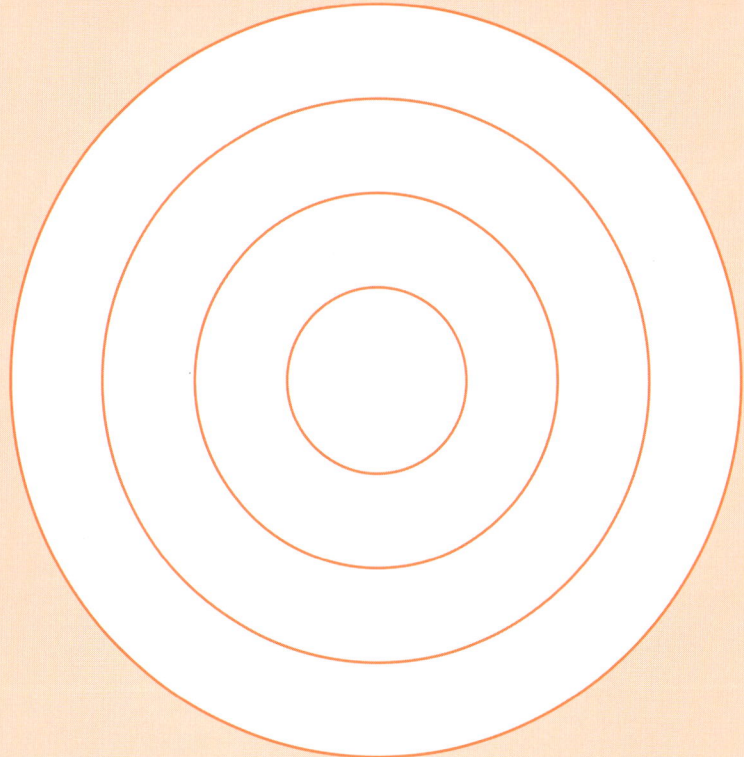

How important

Complete the table below.

- Briefly summarise the importance of each factor in changing the cattle industry in the years c.1876–c.1895.
- Make a decision about the overall importance of each factor, giving a brief explanation for each choice.

Factor	Importance	Decisive	Important	Quite important
The development of cattle ranching				
Refrigerated railcars				
The winter of 1886–87				
The changing role of cowboys				

2 Conflict and tension

2.1 Extent of solutions to problems of law and order

To tackle the constant problem of lawlessness, sheriffs and marshals were hired to solve a town's problems. Their role was to maintain law and order, arrest troublemakers, resolve disputes and imprison offenders.

The Earps and the OK Corral, 1881

The mining town of Tombstone, Arizona, suffered from lawlessness. As the town grew, rivalry between mining companies increased. Virgil Earp was hired as town marshal; he brought with him his brothers **Wyatt** and Morgan to tackle the lawlessness. Local groups of men enjoyed drinking and gambling, which often led to violence. A dispute developed between the Earps, and local outlaws such as the Clantons, Doc Holliday and the Cowboys. In the end, the Earps won a gunfight (the famous shootout at the OK **Corral**) and Tombstone became a more peaceful town.

2.2 The range wars

As homesteaders, miners, hunters and ranchers flooded on to the Great Plains, they came into conflict with each other.

The Lincoln County War, 1878

This conflict was sparked by the murder of John Tunstall by the House Cowboys. **Billy the Kid** and others set about avenging his murder. Thirty people were killed before it was over.

The Johnson County War, 1892

Homesteaders and small ranchers settling in Wyoming came into conflict with **cattle barons** over land ownership. The first killing took place in 1889, and battles continued into 1892. Trials were held but the courts ran out of money and no charges were brought; however, the cattle barons were never as powerful again.

2.3 Conflict with the Plains Indians

The Great Sioux War, 1876–77

A military expedition to protect railway surveyors and gold prospectors in the Black Hills ultimately triggered a war with the Sioux. The government made an offer to buy the Black Hills from the Sioux, which they rejected. The military campaign that followed led to the Battle of the Little Bighorn.

The Battle of the Little Bighorn, 1876

This was a great victory for the Plains Indians and a serious defeat for the US Army. The Native Americans had superior numbers and Winchester repeating rifles, and **General Custer** made some strategic mistakes despite warnings from his scouts. The defeat shocked American citizens, who demanded further military campaigns against the Plains Indians.

Key terms

Cattle barons Businessmen and landowners who possessed great power or influence through the operation of a large ranch with many beef cattle

Corral A pen for livestock, especially cattle or horses, on a farm or ranch

---

Key individuals

Billy the Kid Born Henry McCarty, and also known as William H. Bonney. He was a gunfighter who participated in New Mexico's Lincoln County War. He was alleged to have killed eight men

General Custer George Armstrong Custer had served with distinction during the Civil War and had previously had victories over the Plains Indians, including defeating the Cheyenne at the Battle of Washita

Wyatt Earp Had various law enforcement roles among other jobs; often regarded as the central figure in the gunfight at Tombstone, although his official role was less significant than that of his brother Virgil, the town's marshal

---

Quick quizzes at **www.hoddereducation.co.uk/myrevisionnotes**

Wounded Knee Massacre, 1890

- On New Year's Day 1889, a Native American holy man received a vision. An Indian Messiah was coming, and if Plains Indians remained peaceful and danced the 'Ghost Dance', then a new world would come where all the white people would disappear and the buffalo would return.

- The Ghost Dance religion spread rapidly across Native American reservations.

- The Ghost Dance was banned, but many Native Americans joined Big Foot, a Plains Indian chief, who was a leader for the Ghost Dance.

- The US Seventh Cavalry caught up with Big Foot and his followers, and took them under guard to a camp at Wounded Knee.

- While the soldiers were removing their weapons, a Sioux warrior resisted and opened fire.

- The soldiers retaliated, and 146 Indians were killed, along with 25 soldiers. Among the dead Native Americans were old men, women and children.

- This massacre marked the end of the plains wars.

✎ How important

Here is an exam-style question:

Explain the importance of the range wars (1878–92).

Below is a grid showing the importance of the range wars. Copy and complete the grid by:

- making a decision about how important each range war was
- briefly explaining each decision.

Factor	Very important	Important	Quite important
The Lincoln County War			
The Johnson County War			

✎ Concentric circles

In the concentric circles opposite, rank order the following reasons for increased tension and conflict in the years 1876–95, from the most important in the middle to the least important on the outside. Explain your decisions.

- the role of sheriffs and marshals
- the range wars
- conflicts with the Plains Indians
- the role of the US Army.

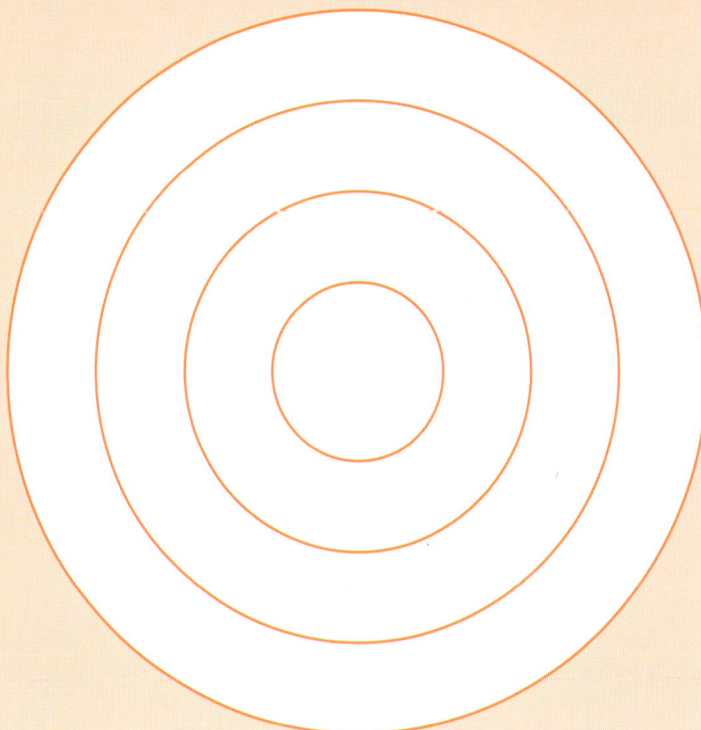

3 The Plains Indians: the destruction of their way of life

3.1 The hunting and extermination of the buffalo

One way to keep the Plains Indians on their reservations was destroy the buffalo, which was the foundation of their nomadic lifestyle. The extermination of the buffalo was a combination of US government policy and other factors. The US military were instructed by the government to kill as many buffalo as they could.

Buffalo hunters killed the animals for their hides, which they could sell to **tanneries** in the East for a good price. The remains of the buffalo, after the hunter took the hide, were collected by homesteaders and crews of professional 'bone pickers' and taken to railroad sidings. These bones were transported East to be manufactured into glue, fertiliser, buttons, combs and knife handles.

3.2 The Plains Indians' life on the reservations

Plains Indians were virtually prisoners on their reservations from the mid-1870s. Many reservations were on poor-quality land, making it difficult to grow food, so the Plains Indians became dependent on government handouts.

Difficulties experienced by Plains Indians

- Some Native American agents, operating as the link between the Plains Indians and the government, were dishonest and stole money (from the US government) that should have gone to the Native Americans for housing, food and medical treatment.
- Many Plains Indians on reservations suffered from diseases such as measles, influenza and whooping cough, which they found difficult to resist.
- Some Indian Nations, for example the Pawnee, adapted to reservation life better than others, as they had been farmers, and were not nomadic hunters like the Sioux.
- Native Americans had little legal status or control.
- Native American religious feasts, dances and ceremonies were banned on the reservations, and this undermined the power that medicine men had within the tribe.
- Many Native American children were sent away to boarding schools, and if parents resisted then food rations (provided by the US government) were withheld.

The reservation effectively damaged the Plains Indians' tribal structure and their self-belief in their ideas about tradition and community.

3.3 Changing government attitudes

- The Indian Appropriations Act 1871 was the most significant piece of US government policy that affected the Plains Indians. This marked the end of their being treated as independent sovereign nations.
- By 1876, the US government was determined to be at peace with the Plains Indian through a policy of forcing them to live on reservations.
- The Dawes General Allotment Act 1887 allowed reservations to be broken up into individual plots, which destroyed the power of Native American chiefs and the tribal structure.

Key term

Tannery A place where animal hides are made into leather; the workshop of a tanner

Revision task

Make a list of the ways in which Plains Indians had their independence limited by the actions and restrictions resulting from government policy.

Exam tip

Ensure that you know how the government attitudes changed from accommodating the Plains Indians to wanting their removal, and the policies which reflected this change.

Memory map

Create a memory map to show the different reasons for the destruction of the Plains Indians' way of life. Add some key words from the information on page 26 and your own knowledge to the diagram opposite. To help you remember the information, you could add small drawings.

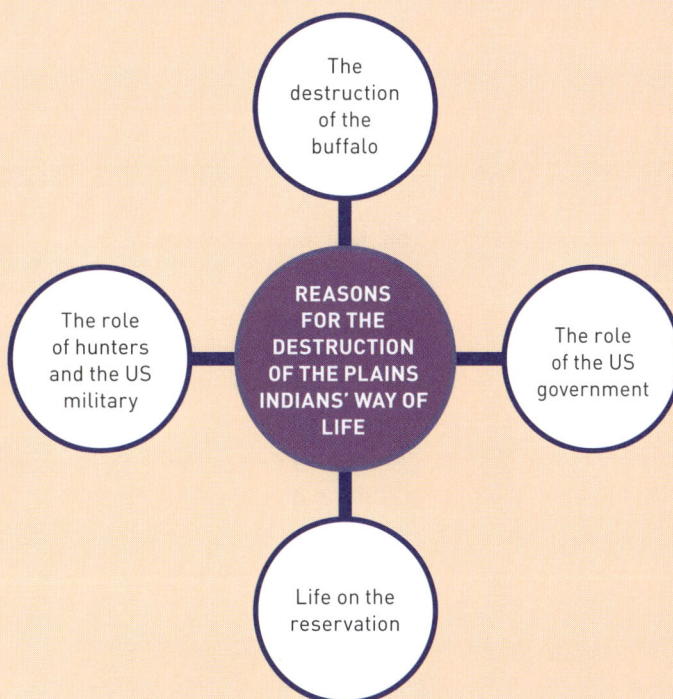

The destruction of the buffalo

The role of hunters and the US military

REASONS FOR THE DESTRUCTION OF THE PLAINS INDIANS' WAY OF LIFE

The role of the US government

Life on the reservation

Improving your answer

Plan an answer to the question below. Compare your plan with that of another student and suggest three ways in which the plan could be improved.

Write a narrative account analysing the destruction of the Plains Indians' way of life.

You may use the following in your answer:
- **The destruction of the buffalo**
- **Life on the reservation**

You **must** also use information of your own.

My plan

Exam technique

Your History GCSE is made up of three exams:

- Paper 1 on a thematic study and historic environment.
- Paper 2 on a British depth study and a period study, in your case The American West c.1835–c.1895.
- Paper 3 on a modern depth study.

For the period study in Paper 2 you have to answer the following types of questions. Each requires you to demonstrate different historical skills:

- **Question 1** is a consequence question in which you have to explain two consequences of a given development or event.
- **Question 2** is a narrative question. You have to write an account which analyses events or developments in the American West c.1835–c.1895 with detail. You can choose to write about the two given events, but you must also write about an event or development of your own.
- **Question 3** is an importance question. You are asked to make a judgement on the importance of two different events or developments, supported by a precise and developed explanation.

The table below gives a summary of the question types for Paper 2 and what you need to do.

Question number	Marks	Key words	You need to...
1	8	Explain **two** consequences of ...	• Ensure you focus on consequence • Fully explain each consequence
2	8	Write a narrative account analysing ... You may use the following in your answer: [two given events/developments] You **must** also use information of your own	• Analyse at least three events/developments • Fully explain each with supporting detail
3	16	Explain **two** of the following: • The importance of ... for the... • The importance of ... for the... • The importance of ... for the...	• Choose two of the three developments • Ensure that you focus on importance • Fully explain its importance using precise evidence

Exam focus

Question 1: Consequence

Below is an example exam-style consequence question. It is worth 8 marks.

Explain two consequences of the Indian Removal Act 1830.

How to answer

1   <u>Underline</u> key points in the question. This will ensure that you focus sharply on what is required.

2   Identify two consequences of the Indian Removal Act 1830.

3   Begin each paragraph by stating the consequence. For example, 'One consequence of the Indian Removal Act 1830 was …'.

4   Give a fully developed explanation about the consequence including precise details.

5   State the second consequence. For example, 'A further consequence of the Indian Removal Act 1830 was …'.

6   Give a fully developed explanation about the second consequence including precise evidence.

Below is a sample answer to another exam-style consequence question with comments around it.

Explain two consequences of the Gold Rush of 1849.

One consequence of the Gold Rush of 1849 was that it attracted miners from all over America and the world, including China. Many took the wagon route across the Great Plains, following the California trail. Others came by sea, having sailed around the southern tip of South America, or via Panama. This type of journey could take between 70 and 84 days. The population of California expanded significantly from around 15,000 in 1848, before the Gold Rush, to nearly 250,000 by 1852.

> The question is focused on through referring to the first consequence.

> A detailed explanation of this consequence is given.

> Precise evidence is given in this explanation.

Another consequence of the Gold Rush of 1849 was that mining towns developed, and to begin with they were lawless. There were no organised forces of law and order, and miners did as they pleased. They settled disputes in their own courts that had no legal basis. They decided on punishments, which ranged from flogging to hanging. Shopkeepers and saloon owners moved to the towns to make money from the miners, and a combination of gambling and alcohol led to violence which was not controlled.

> The question is focused on through referring to the second consequence.

> A detailed explanation of the second consequence is given.

> Precise evidence is given in this explanation.

Exam focus activity

Below is an exam-style consequence question with two answers. Which is the better answer? Give three reasons why.

Explain two consequences of the impact of the Civil War on the settlement of the West.

ANSWER 1

In 1861, a civil war broke out between the northern and the southern states of the USA. During the Civil War there was great destruction to towns and cities, factories were damaged, crops destroyed and miles of railway tracks were torn up. As a consequence of this war, the process of moving west and settling was delayed, as people could not easily make the journey. Also during the war, regular troops were withdrawn from the West and this impacted on the Plains Indians.

ANSWER 2

One consequence of the Civil War on the settlement of the West was that when the war was over thousands of men were demobilised and returned to their homes. Many had been changed by the experience of the war, and looked for a new start. Moving and settling west seemed to offer this new start. In 1862, President Lincoln had signed the Homestead Act, and this allowed anyone who had not taken up arms against the USA to claim 160 acres of land for free. This was the government encouraging further settlement in the West. This was added to in 1866 with the Southern Homestead Act, which was designed to encourage freed slaves and whites who had not supported the Confederacy to take up ownership of land in the West.

Another consequence was as the war ended, the US government encouraged further settlement in the West by offering land grants to railroad companies to rebuild damaged tracks and build new railroads. In 1865, two tracks raced forward: in the West the Central Pacific Railroad, and in the East the Union Pacific Railroad. The completion of these railroads helped with the increased settlement of homesteaders, allowing them to carry equipment and supplies to their new homes. It also encouraged the growth of the cattle industry, and cow towns grew.

1.

2.

3.

Question 2: Narrative account

Below is an example of an exam-style narrative question which is worth 8 marks.

Write a narrative account analysing why the Mormons migrated west across America.

How to answer

- Look for the key points in the question and underline them.

- You can choose to write about the two key people given in the question and another reason of your own, or write entirely about reasons of your own.

- If you write about the two key people in the question, make sure you write about at least three reasons. Including three reasons is important because you *must bring in a reason of your own*.

- Ensure that you give detail about each of the reasons you write about.

- Use linking words between each reason and the next. Try to use phrases such as 'this led to', 'as a result of this'.

> You may use the following information in your answer:
> - **The role of Joseph Smith**
> - **The role of Brigham Young**
>
> You **must** also use information of your own.

Below is a sample answer to this exam-style narrative question with comments around it.

One reason why the Mormons migrated westwards across America was because of Joseph Smith. Mormons were followers of Joseph Smith because as a teenager he began having religious experiences and he claimed an angel told him about two buried gold plates. Smith said that he had found these plates, dug them up and translated them. This became the Book of Mormon. Smith told his followers to start building God's Kingdom, in America, and prepare for the second coming of Jesus Christ. As the Mormon religion grew, many non-Mormons became hostile and Smith told his followers to move to Kirtland in Ohio. As a community, the Mormons worked hard and became prosperous, even during the depression of the 1930s. This also made them unpopular, as many people resented them and were envious and jealous of them. This forced them to move to Missouri. Smith also preached that God had told him that Mormons could have more than one wife. Smith was denounced as a false prophet, and in June 1845 was attacked and murdered.

> Using the words of the question gives immediate focus.

> There is a developed analysis of the role of Joseph Smith, using precise details.

As a consequence of Smith's murder, a new Mormon leader, Brigham Young, came to the forefront and stated that Mormons could not live alongside non-Mormons. He said they should move to the area around the Great Salt Lake, east of the Rocky Mountains. He chose this area because of its isolation and its unattractiveness, hoping that no other people would want to settle there. Gradually Salt Lake City developed as a Mormon settlement. The Mormons became self-sufficient in food.

> A link is made between Smith and Young.

> There is a developed analysis of the role of Young.

Another reason why the Mormons migrated west across America was that wherever the Mormons lived, they were accused of being sympathetic towards the Plains Indians, and against slavery. Local settlers often caused riots in protest against them and troops were needed to settle the disorder. However, it was the Mormons who were always blamed for these disturbances. As a consequence, the Mormons were forced to move to Nauvoo, Illinois.

> A third reason for migration west is introduced.

> There is a developed analysis of the third reason.

✎ 'Through the eyes' of the examiner

Below is an exam-style narrative question with part of a sample answer. It would be useful to look at this an answer 'through the eyes' of an examiner. The examiner will look for the following:

- three reasons
- clear links between the reasons
- an explanation of each reason.

You need to:

- Highlight words or phrases which show that the answer has focused on the question.
- Underline where attempts are made to show links between one reason and the next.
- In the margin write a word or phrase which sums up each specific explanation as it appears.

Write a narrative account analysing the main ways in which the US government destroyed the Plains Indians' way of life.

> **You may use the following information in your answer:**
> - the reservation
> - the building of military forts
>
> **You must also use information of your own.**

The policy of relocating Plains Indians to reservations as developed by the US government was the main way in which the government destroyed the Plains Indians' way of life. Before living on reservations, Plains Indians had been nomadic, and followed the buffalo in order to sustain their way of life. This changed with the onset of the reservation. President Grant's Peace Policy of 1869 depended on the Plains Indians living on reservations and taking up farming, and only leaving the reservation to hunt buffalo. However, as the US government never protected the buffalo for Native American hunting alone, buffalo hunters were allowed to hunt the animal at will, and this led to the virtual extermination of the buffalo. In 1887, the Dawes General Allotment Act allowed communal reservation land to be broken up into individual plots. This was intended to completely destroy the power of the Plains Indians' chiefs and their tribal structure.

Restricting the Plains Indians to designated reservations inevitably led to disagreement, confusion and conflict. A series of conflicts between the Plains Indians and settlers led to US Army intervention which then led to some major battles between some of the Plains Indian tribes. After the Battle of the Little Bighorn, the US government took the decision to build forts and send in troops and spend money to finally defeat the Sioux and its allies. These forts allowed the US Army to confine the Plains Indians to their reservations by regular patrols and observation of their activities. These forts were strategically placed to ensure that no one left the reservation.

✎ Adding a third event

The answer above does not include a third event. What would you choose as a third event and why? Try completing the answer, remembering to add details to support your chosen event.

Question 3: Importance

Below is an exam-style importance question.

Explain two of the following:

- The importance of the horse to the Plains Indians' way of life.
- The importance of the 'mountain men' in the early settlement of the West.
- The importance of the railways in the development of the West.

How to answer

- You must choose **two** of these three developments. Your choice should be based on the two you feel provide greater opportunity for you to focus on *importance*.

- For the two you have chosen underline key points in the question. This will ensure that you focus sharply on what the question wants you to write about.

- Remember for each development that you choose, the focus of the question is its **importance** for a further factor and/or event.

Below is a part of a sample answer to this exam-style importance question with comments around it.

The horse was very important to the Plains Indians' way of life. Originally there were no horses in America, and it was Spanish invaders who had introduced them to the continent. The Pueblo Indians of Mexico revolted against the Spanish and captured their horses. Horses were then traded between the Indian Nations. With horses, the Indian Nations, like the Sioux and Cheyenne, were able to move on to the Great Plains to live and hunt buffalo. They gave up farming and became nomadic, all because of the horse. This then allowed the Plains Indians to live in smaller bands. The horse also became a means of transporting the home (tipi) and family members. The horse also changed the nature of warfare. Plains Indian warriors could now travel greater distances and raid further afield, allowing them to steal even more horses. Horses also led to greater horsemanship among Plains Indian warriors, and this became an important measure of their status and bravery. Horses became so vital to the Plains Indians' way of life that ownership of them counted towards an individual's wealth, status and prestige.

> There is an immediate focus on the key word of the question: importance.

> A developed explanation is given using precise details.

> The importance of the horse is focused on again.

> Judgement is made about the importance of the horse to the way of life.

✎ Exam focus activity

The answer above does not include a second development. What would you choose as the second important development and why? Try completing the answer, remembering to add details to support your chosen development.

Revision techniques

HOW CAN I REMEMBER IT ALL?

We all learn in different ways and if you're going to be successful in your revision you need to work out the ways that work best for you. Remember that revision doesn't have to be dull and last for hours at a time – but it is really important you do it! The highest grades are awarded to students who have consistently excellent subject knowledge and this only comes with solid revision.

Method 1: 'Brain dumps'

These are particularly useful when done every so often – it's never too early to start! Take a big piece of paper or even a whiteboard and write down everything you can remember about the topic you are revising, one of the units or even the whole History course. You could write down:

- dates
- names of key individuals
- key events
- important place names
- anything else you can remember.

Once you're satisfied you can't remember any more, use different colours to highlight or underline the words in groups. For example, when revising the problem of the Plains Indians you might choose to underline all the mentions that relate to the causes in red and to the effects in blue.

You could extend this task by comparing your brain dump with that of a friend. The next time you do it, try setting yourself a shorter time limit and see if you can write down more.

Method 2: Learning walks

Make use of your space! Write down key facts and place them around your home, where you will see them every day. Make an effort to read the facts whenever you walk past them. You might decide to put information on the conflicts between settlers and Plains Indians, with the idea of the government tackling lawlessness.

Method 3: 'Distilling'

Memory studies show that we retain information better if we revisit it regularly. This means that revising the information once is not necessarily going to help it stay in your brain. Going back over the facts at intervals of less than a week leads to the highest retention of facts.

To make this process streamlined, try 'distilling' your notes. Start by reading over the notes you've completed in class or in this revision guide; two days later, read over them again, and this time write down everything you didn't remember. If you repeat this process enough you will end up with hardly any facts left to write down, because they will all be stored in your brain, ready for the exam!

Method 4: Using your downtime

There are always little pockets of time through the day which aren't much good for anything: bus journeys, queues, ad breaks in TV programmes, waiting for the bath to run and so on. If you added all these minutes up it would probably amount to quite a lot of time, which can be put to good use for revision.

Instead of having to carry around your notes, though, make use of something you carry around with you already. Most of us have a phone that can take pictures and record voice memos, or an iPod or something similar.

Photograph key sections of this book and read over them.

Record yourself reading information so that you can listen back over it – while you're playing football, before you go to sleep, or at any other time.

Access the quizzes that go with this book at www.hoddereducation.co.uk/myrevisionnotes

Answers

Page 5: Organising knowledge

Key factor	Impact on Plains Indians' beliefs and way of life
The role of men, women and old people	Plains Indian men were the hunter-gathers, warriors and protectors of the tribe. Women prepared the food and were the homemakers. Old people gave advice and passed on the history of the tribe
The horse	The horse was used for hunting, a means of transport and warfare. The number of horses an individual had gave them prestige and status. Good horsemanship also indicated bravery
The buffalo	The buffalo was very important to the Plains Indians. They hunted them and used their meat for food, their hides for clothing and their horns for ladles and spoons. The heart of the buffalo was put in the ground to give new life to the herd
The land	The land was sacred for Plains Indians. They believed that they came from the earth, just like plants and animals
War	Plains Indians saw war as a means to an end. It was about rivalry over hunting grounds and living space. War allowed them to prove their bravery and gain social status

Page 7: How important

Factor	Key features	Decisive	Important	Quite important
Living as a band			Plains Indians spent the year travelling, hunting and camping as a band	
The horse		As well as hunting, the horse was used as a means of transport for home and family, changed warfare, and confirmed the status and prestige of a Plains Indian		
The buffalo		Hunted as a source of food and clothing, it also had a mystical status seen in buffalo dances		
Belief in spirits		Plains Indians believed that all living things has spirits		
Attitude to war			War was about rivalry and hunting rights, as well as living space	
The role of the US government			The relationship between Plains Indians and the US government varied from friendship and cooperation to hostility and open war	

Page 9: Concentric circles

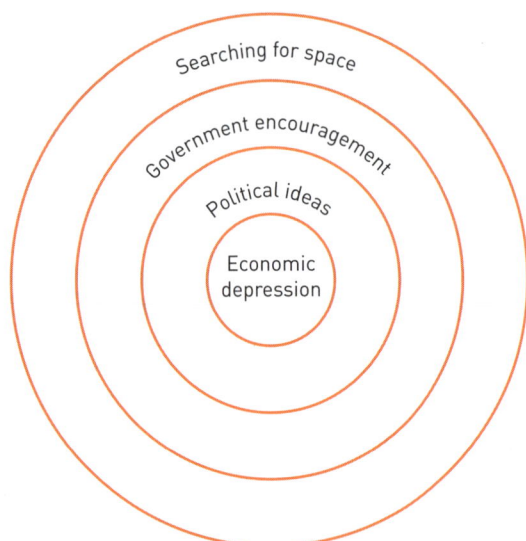

Concentric circles (outer to inner):
- Searching for space
- Government encouragement
- Political ideas
- Economic depression

Explanation

1 The impact of the economic depression meant that many people needed a new start. They looked for new land to settle on so that they could start a new life for themselves and their families.

2 The idea of 'Manifest Destiny' convinced many people that it was their God-given duty and role in life to spread 'civilisation' and democracy across the continent to the regions of Oregon and California.

3 The US government passed legislation which encouraged and allowed settlers to stake a claim for land after living on it for fourteen months.

4 Mountain men and early settlers sent back tales of how much land and space was available in Oregon, and they also told of sunny valleys and a climate that was ideal for farming.

Page 11: Organising knowledge

Factors	Major problem	Minor problem
The time migration took	Often took much longer than originally planned	
Encountering hazards	Trying to take short cuts led to problems	Many stuck to the established trails
Food supplies	Not fully supplied for a journey that took longer than planned, and especially if it lasted into the winter months	
Being unprepared	Lack of the necessary clothing and equipment to survive the long journey	
Increasing the population of an area		Led to some minor conflicts and disagreements

Page 15: Understanding the chronology

Date	Event
1861–65	E The American Civil War
1865	F Building of the Central Pacific Railroad started
1866	B Southern Homestead Act

Date	Event
1869	A Completion of the transcontinental railroad
1873	D Timber Culture Act
1877	C Desert Land Act

Page 17: Consequences and importance

Problem	Consequences	Importance
Location of their land	No forests on the plains	No wood for fuel, heating or cooking
High winds	Prairie fires stoked by high winds; soil eroded from growth areas	Fires destroyed crops; soil erosion led to poor farming land
Low rainfall	Drought in the summer	Caused crop damage and low-yield harvest
Natural hazards	Prairie fires, grasshoppers	Caused great crop damage
Cold winters	Freezing temperatures	Life uncomfortable during the winter months
Ownership of weapons	Most people owned a gun for protection	Led to breakdown in law and order, no consequences for violent action

Page 17: Organising knowledge

Factor	1862	1877
Railroad transportation	Opened up opportunities for settlers	Completion of new railroads for further expansion west
Farming	The open range	The end of the open range
Law and order	Out of control because of weapons, bank robbery and train robbery	The consequences of range wars
Land acquisition rights	Affected by the discovery of gold	US government opened up areas for further expansion west .

Page 19: Identifying consequences

Statement	Cause	Event	Consequence
The Civil War played a part in the growth of the cattle industry		✓	
Cattle ranchers who had fought in the war returned to find that their herds had grown significantly in size			✓
Cattle were worth less after the war and had to be sold			✓
Cow towns emerged and became prosperous			✓
The work of the cowboy changed as they now drove cattle to a town for transportation			✓

Page 21: Consequences and importance

Factor	Consequences	Importance
The advance of the railroad	The advancing railroads cut lines across their hunting grounds and scared animals away	An important source of many aspects of Plains Indian life, the buffalo, had their living space threatened
Cattle ranches	Cattle on the open range were in direct competition for grazing land with the buffalo	Any spread of ranching decreased the area that buffalo herds could roam and feed on, which impacted on the Plains Indians' way of life
Gold prospecting	The rush of people into areas with possible gold deposits frightened away the animals that the Plains Indians hunted	Loss of animals for hunting and more people meant increased tension
Indian Appropriations Act 1871	Ended the treatment of Plains Indians as independent sovereign nations	Being considered as individual US citizens was not what most Plains Indians wanted
The Cheyenne Wars 1864–67	The wars ultimately led to the Arapaho and Cheyenne moving to reservations	Reservation life was restrictive and impacted on their traditional way of life

Page 23: Concentric circles

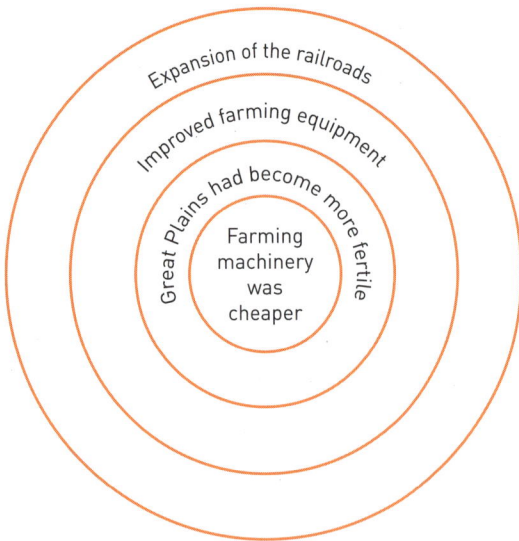

Concentric circles (from outer to inner):
- Expansion of the railroads
- Improved farming equipment
- Great Plains had become more fertile
- Farming machinery was cheaper

Explanation

1 Homesteaders were able to buy a wide range of farming machinery, for example binders, reapers and threshers, at cheaper prices, and they could buy spares.

2 The Great Plains had become more fertile and many homesteaders prospered as improved methods of farming and access to equipment meant that they could cultivate more land, and as a consequence land became more fertile and yielded more crops.

3 James Oliver improved the steel plough, enabling farmers to cultivate more land. Increased crop yields led to more money, which then led to further investment in better technology.

4 The expansion of the railroads brought about significant improvements in farming, as new ideas, methods and equipment could be transported west more quickly.

Page 23: How important

Factor	Importance	Decisive	Important	Quite important
The development of cattle ranching	Improved the quality of cattle and meat and meant that farmers earned more money		Yes	
Refrigerated railcars	Meant that meat could be preserved and transported over greater distances	Yes		
The winter of 1886–87	The winter of 1886–87 was so cold that thousands of cattle died. The 'open range' had had its best days and the boom was over	Yes		
The changing role of cowboys	Open range was replaced by smaller ranches, and cowboys' lives were never the same again	Yes		

Page 25: How important

Factor	Very important	Important	Quite important
The Lincoln County War		Billy the Kid became famous and was on the run from the authorities	
The Johnson County War	The cattle barons never had the same power again		

Page 25: Concentric circles

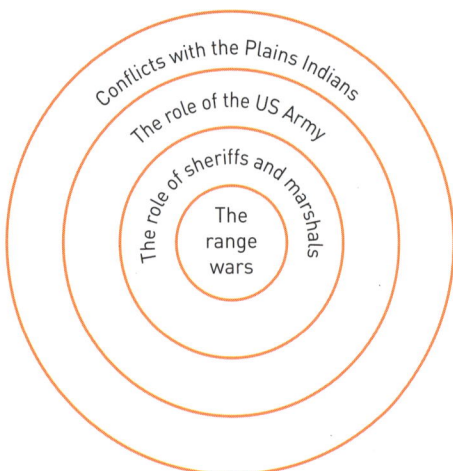

Concentric circles (from outer to inner):
- Conflicts with the Plains Indians
- The role of the US Army
- The role of sheriffs and marshals
- The range wars

Explanation

1 The range wars led to constant breakdowns in law and order, and fights between rival gangs.

2 The role of sheriffs and marshals, while important in trying to control law and order, created further friction and fighting.

3 The US Army increasingly became involved in breakdowns of law and order, and often over-reacted, and this created further problems and tension.

4 There were continued problems with the Plains Indians, although their settlement in reservations had led to a decrease in tension; however, the US Army and settlers still came into contact with them and this led, sometimes, to conflict.